Bilingual Edition
LET'S LOOK AT FEELINGS™
Edición Bilingüe

What I Look Like When I Am
Happy

Cómo me veo cuando estoy
contento

Heidi Johansen
Traducción al español:
María Cristina Brusca

The Rosen Publishing Group's
PowerStart Press™ & **Editorial Buenas Letras**™
New York

1

For Daniel Ernesto

Published in 2004 by The Rosen Publishing Group, Inc.
29 East 21st Street, New York, NY 10010

First Edition

Book Design: Kim Sonsky
Photo Credits: All photos by Maura B. McConnell.

Library of Congress Cataloging-in-Publication Data

Johansen, Heidi Leigh.
[What I look like when I am happy. Spanish & English]
What I look like when I am happy = Como me veo cuando estoy contento / Heidi Leigh Johansen ; translated by Maria Cristina Brusca.
    p. cm. – (Let's look at feelings)
Summary: Describes what different parts of the face look like when a person is happy. Spanish and English.
Includes index.
  ISBN 1-4042-7506-1 (library binding)
1. Happiness in children—Juvenile literature. [1. Happiness. 2. Facial expression. 3. Emotions. 4. Spanish language material—Bilingual.] I. Title: Como me veo cuando estoy contento. II. Title. III. Series.
  BF723.H37J6418 2004
  152.4'2-dc21

                                                    2003009075

Manufactured in the United States of America

Due to the changing nature of Internet links, PowerKids Press has developed an online list of Web sites related to the subject of this book. This site is updated regularly. Please use this link to access the list:

www.buenasletraslinks.com/llafe/contento/

Contents

1 I Am Happy   4
2 My Face   6
Words to Know   24
Index   24

Contenido

1 Estoy contento   4
2 Mi rostro   6
Palabras que debes saber   24
Índice   24

I am happy.

Estoy contento.

My mouth makes a smile
when I am happy.

Cuando estoy contenta
mi boca dibuja una sonrisa.

When I am happy I smile with my mouth closed.

Cuando estoy contenta sonrío con la boca cerrada.

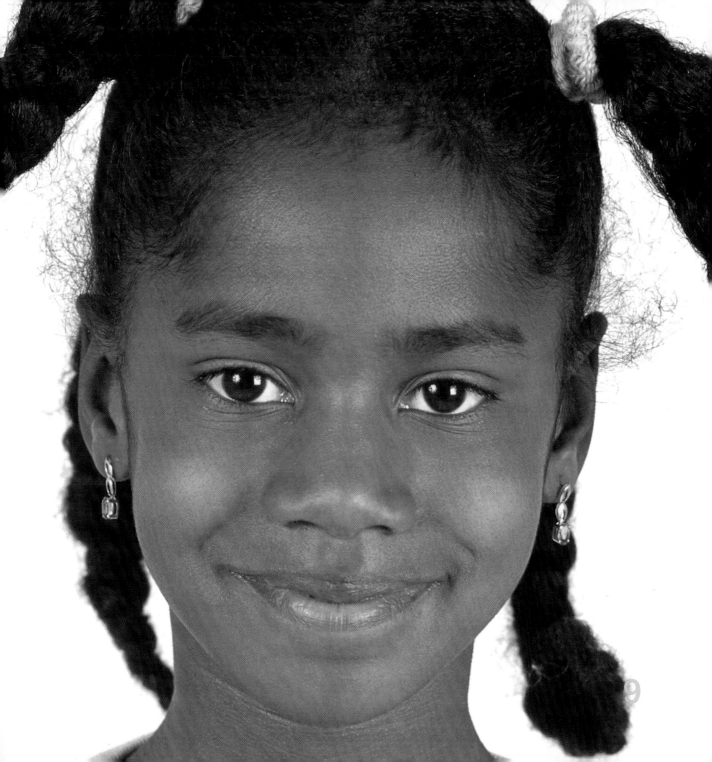

You can see my teeth when
I am happy.

_____

Mis dientes se asoman
cuando estoy contenta.

11

I laugh when I am happy.

Me río cuando estoy contento.

When I am happy my
cheeks look round.

Mis mejillas se ponen
redondas cuando
estoy contenta.

15

There are lines on both sides of my mouth when I am happy.

Cuando estoy contento se dibujan líneas a los costados de mi boca.

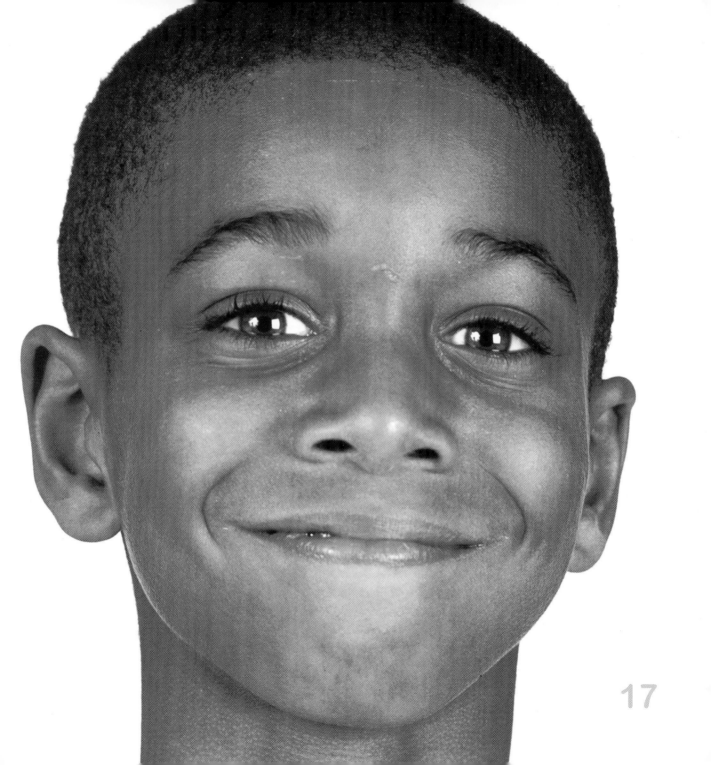

17

There are lines by my eyes when I am happy.

Cuando estoy contento se forman líneas alrededor de mis ojos.

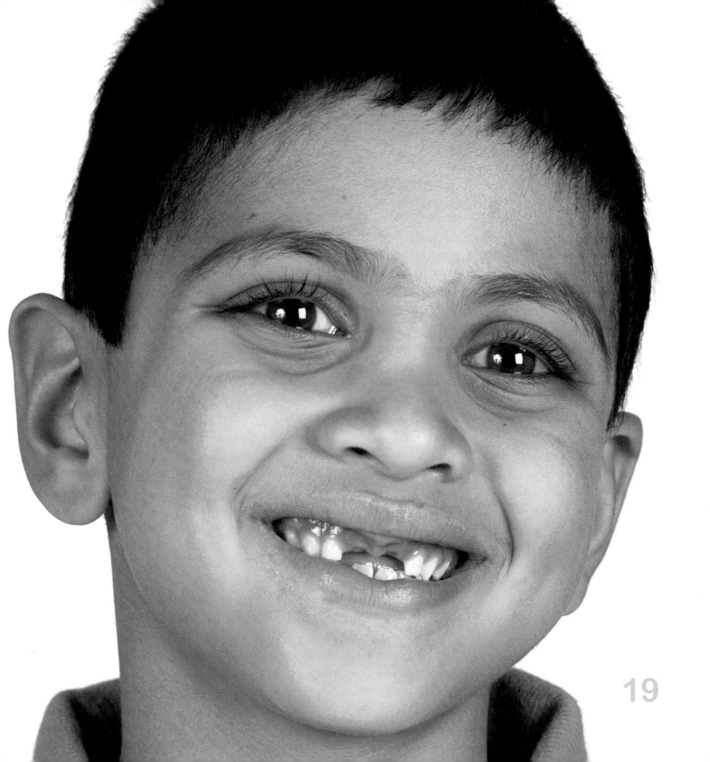

19

There are lines on my nose
when I am happy.

Mi nariz tiene muchas
líneas cuando
estoy contento.

21

This is what I look like when I am happy.

Así me veo cuando estoy contenta.

23

Words to Know
Palabras que debes saber

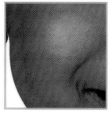

cheek
mejilla

laugh
risa

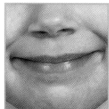

mouth
boca

nose
nariz

smile
sonrisa

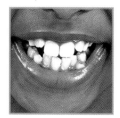

teeth
dientes

Index

C
cheeks, 14

E
eyes, 18

L
laugh, 12

M
mouth, 6, 8, 16

S
smile, 6, 8

T
teeth, 10

Índice

B
boca, 6, 8, 16

D
dientes, 10

M
mejillas, 14

O
ojos, 18

R
río, 12

S
sonrisa, 6, 8

24